The Spoken World

HAGIOS
PRESS

The Spoken World

Harold Rhenisch

HAGIOS PRESS
Box 33024 Cathedral PO
Regina SK   S4T 7X2
www.hagiospress.com

A CIP catalogue record for this book is available from Library and Archives Canada.
ISBN 978-1-926710-12-9

Edited by Paul Wilson.
Designed and typeset by Donald Ward.
Cover photograph by Marcia M. Willis.
Cover design by Tania Wolk, Go Giraffe Go Inc.
Set in Adobe Caslon Pro.
Printed and bound in Canada.

The publishers gratefully acknowledge the assistance of the Saskatchewan Arts Board, The Canada Council for the Arts, and the Cultural Industries Development Fund (Saskatchewan Department of Culture, Youth & Recreation) in the production of this book.

Contents

A Word of Welcome

ONCE THERE WERE TWO MEN TALKING. One was the poet, shaman, witch, and celebrant called Robin Skelton. He died in 1997. Then there was just one.

Robin left me signposts, written in a language of symbol and suggestion we called poetry, yet his last words to me were "the poetry does not matter." It sounded like a complete negation of his life, but then he added, "But I don't know how else we are going to teach our children how to think." It took me ten years to realize that he was passing the conversation on to me.

The conversation that forms this book took place five years later, in 2002 — four years after Robin's daughters asked me to edit his posthumous manuscripts and a selected version of his works. The posthumous book, *Facing the Light*, followed, and the selected poems, *In This Poem I Am*, but first came this book — a series of messages between Robin and me, or between two sides of myself, one called Robin and one called Harold, or just an embodiment of the space Robin and I formed between each other in friendship and common purpose.

When I met Robin back in 1978, I knew a lot about trees and wind and the desert stars, but I was new to the city. In fact I was new to the whole 20th century. I had been raised by pear and apple trees in British Columbia's Similkameen Valley — nominally a part of Canada but really a part of the British Empire, with a strong dose of the lost German Empire for good measure. Coming to Victoria, and the world, was an emigration. Robin had emigrated from England fifteen years earlier, and was going the other way, into the earth. Victoria was halfway for both of us. I had learned to write poetry by pruning apple trees by starlight, and saw in the mountains and rivers my own identity and consciousness. It is what Robin wanted in his deepest heart. What I wanted was the world.

Robin saw this, and kept suggesting to his wife Sylvia that she publish my work. Sylvia ran a small press, Pharos Press, which published poetry that worshipped the Goddess or otherwise invoked the earth's power. Susan Musgrave and Sean Virgo's *Kiskatinaw Songs*, for example, found their first public voice through Pharos Press. With my work, however, Sylvia always hesitated, and in Robin's matriarchal world her word was final.

I didn't see what Robin was going on about at all. To me, my poems were poems like any others written by anyone else in the 1970s: individual, confessional, meditative, imagistic, and narrative, often all at the same time. My models were Rilke, Pound, Yates, and Purdy. I lived in a time past gods and goddesses, informed by the miracle of the university and its library, and the baroque, textured world of literature it fostered. Sylvia saw that clearly. Robin did not, but nonetheless with a light touch he guided me, often well and sometimes poorly, out of my earth and my deafness into poetry and the community of men and women in this world. He did all that even though at the same time the poetry was drawing him more and more rapidly away from that world. I suspect that for him this conversation was bittersweet, and that he treated it with great care.

Robin had begun his writing life by studying literature. It was only in his mid-40s that he discovered a more spiritual path, and the Old Religion. Over the next decade, he went on to reinterpret witchcraft as a form of poetry made with the elements of the earth. Without mentioning a word of his intent to me, he used my earth-poetry, and no doubt that of others, as a tool for finding his way. At the same time, he cast healing spells and exorcised ghosts. In fact, the poems that he wrote in the 1970s are all largely spells, shamanic journeys, and utterances spoken in the dark, fulfilling a self-appointed task of merging literary and incantatory traditions. I used his poetry to much the same end.

Then, in my mid-40s, at the same age at which Robin found his non-textual poetry, I wrote this book, that gives body to our readings of each other. When I was done, I had walked past the last of Robin's signposts — except one. A major signpost on this journey was erected the last time I saw Robin, in early 1997, when I showed him a manuscript of poetry that embodied the world as an image of consciousness. I used the word "eternity" for the timeless present that day. It was pretentious, I know, but to be fair I just wanted to keep the conversation growing, even while I saw Robin dwindling away. It is hard for a young man to comprehend death. I was doing my best.

Robin was characteristically patient. "We all live in eternity," he said, "but we live there alone." About my manuscript he said, "You have everything right, but I can't hear the music in it, and if I can't hear the music I don't trust it. It isn't finished." He was right. I was still thinking that I was directing my poems, that experience could be deepened by a context of ideas, without the ideas being transformed by the experience. I had not yet learned to listen, and to differentiate what I heard from what I thought I heard.

Consciousness of Robin's intent came to me slowly — that we come from the elements and return to the elements, and in all of this vast stretch of time and space there is one point, this temporal, material earth, where we can meet, and touch, suffer, love, and learn. It lasts a brief time, and then blows away like spray off a wave — as Robin did. As I will someday, too. And you.

In this dialogue of identity, the roles of teacher and student are blurred. It wasn't so much that I shared much of Robin's metaphysics but that he and I found our philosophies and metaphysics together, on both sides of the silence that is the world and which is so mysterious and unapproachable to men of words but is easy enough for children and dogs, and which comes inevitably to the dying. This metaphor, of a reader and a poet sitting on opposite sides of silence, unable to touch except through the words that somehow pass through that space between them, was originally Robin's, not mine. He had inherited it from the Scottish poet W. S. Graham. In turn, Graham had inherited the tradition from James Joyce, who got it somewhere between the Jesuits of Dublin and the equally argumentative but less earnest Parisians among whom he lived his life in exile. There is a conversation. This book stands within it, but represents neither its beginning nor its end. It has been going on for as long as there have been names for the world.

Sometimes, however, something happens to this conversation. After a long time of talking, its speakers begin to suspect that they have become the words they use. Later yet, these poets — for that is what they are now — sometimes discover that by living in these words they have wandered into the spaces between them, that there is no going back, and that there is no longer any difference between the world and the book. There is nothing mysterious about this process. All conversations lead in these directions, and although most get interrupted by the intents and needs of the speakers and the bewildering storms of the world, and remain a poor substitute for touch, it is our art as humans to find each other in this way.

When I wrote these poems, I found that some of them were in my voice, and some in Robin's; some were addressed to me from Robin, and others were addressed to him. I tried to sort that out, but finally removed the names when I discovered that each poem in my voice was also in his, and each in his was also in mine, and that they could also all be read as ciphers for Robin's life, passed on through the spells that were his poems, and for my life, too — quite literally spoken to the "you" you are when you enter them. These poems are about the act of reading and of being read, in a country in which identity is shared.

Here are a few signposts for your journey into these pages. The house was in Oak Bay. It had a big King apple tree set off from its north wall, an apricot tree on the south side, and a ghost in the maid's room upstairs. The spells were cast to heal broken bones and broken hearts, to bring children into this world and to bring lovers together. The elements are salt, fire, breath, and the wine that binds them together. Robin saw the world as the story of the goddess and her stag-horned consort, played out millions of times in an eternal present that we call our individual lives. The cigarettes and the whisky are what killed Robin — his breath and his laughter and the deep pool he looked into when he lost himself. For that time, they were the usual thing. *Who's Afraid of Virginia Woolf?* was written for Robin's generation. The classrooms are North American classrooms in which Robin wrestled with death. When he wrote of them, in an attempt at becoming Robert Lowell, his house and his identity became the university itself. By 1970, university politics had pretty much cured him of this affectation. The city is an image of the body as a social place given shape and form by houses, shops, parks, and streets. The breath is the spirit moving into and out of the body. The door is where Robin greeted you and welcomed you in from the world, and where he blessed you on your journey back out into it again. It is a place of great ceremony. The fire is the fire. The moors are a high, treeless landscape Robin walks across to meet himself walking the other way. They are also where consciousness has walked most often since it began, on the ancient road between the stars. It could be Siberia, or the Canadian Arctic, or my own British Columbian grasslands. I do not understand it; all I know is I meet Robin there, and myself; it is a place in poetry; and when I walk along the mid-Fraser River and up the benches into the Chilcotin I walk through my self.

Now I stand at the door, and open it, and welcome you in.

Closing the Gap

I knock on the door to let me in
and tip my hat and scuff

my shoes as I cross the lintel and greet
the man, half ghost, half spell,

who shakes my hand and claps my back.
He once was you. You have forgotten that.

He takes my coat and gives me drink
and talks of souls who find no rest

on autumn earth. He has gathered here
the shapes of thought, the spheres of art.

Feathers, candles, salt, black bread
answer quiet with words and words with me,

who he has answered, who I have called
across the rain and through the door

to this cold comfort and the lure of words
that will release what has been bound

and bind that which is lost. Found,
I find at last that I am home.

The door that closes
is the door that closing opens.

Going Back

I should think it strange
to speak to you like this. We have talked

across a table piled high with words
and the sacrifice of a flask

of Jameson's and one squat candle.
Now you have gone along

the road into — where? Fog?
The moors your poems set as lures?

The walking stick they placed
in your jewelled hand? We should say fog,

with the heather turning bronze
against black scree; it may be a forest

when I come the other way,
with deer between the pines, or a spit

curling north into the Pacific. Such
spells are as natural as breathing,

a comfortable coat I slip on to walk,
in the hope of meeting you, whistling.

I try it now. When I catch you up I look behind
and see myself, going back.

All Hallows

Those nights a generation past
when you sat at your dark window
with a fire burning outside your kitchen
and I fled all sleep to walk above the sea
are still the nights I am, the night
my children's children will find
when the bed is cold, frost on the glass,
and belief falls from the trees.
What stays with me above pungent leaves
is how old I felt, older than the heartsick sea
that lunged beneath the cliff. I thought
every word I wrote was new. Every word is older
than the falling stars and the calls of humpback whales.
It is I who am younger every year as I approach, or leave,
the first word of the world. The fire of age,
the slow and halting flame that burns
in ash drenched with rain, the blackened
ends of sticks where grass is scraped aside to earth,
the tides of rising mountains and buckling cliffs
are now or then? Rain does fall as strands
of music and apricot leaves all go dark at once
as clouds pass, but return to light only slowly, in gusts.
The world is dancing, but to what tune?

What should I say here in this dark
as I meet myself leaving the fire — now,
grey-haired, as I am, going back? That the ground
I walk upon is only love, that the sun
is not in the sky but within me and does
not rise and does not set? That I do?
That would be too much all at once.
That outside the window stars rain on the earth,
burn brightly for a moment, and then go out?

I spelled reverence in words. All my years
are between the boards that bind
the books, the late nights writing to forget the words
which replace sleep and make some sense
of love that has no sense and death, that does.
Now I must bow within the books and walk
the fields within submission,
where land breaks finally above the sea
and waves roar up, birds cry, stones sing.

Robin

I dreaded that first robin so.
He ate the worm that I would catch
to catch the trout that I would eat

before I rose from my twisted bed
in the twisted house I built with Jack,
inside out with a loft for birds

to sing at dawn and sleep at night.
The northern sky is green and cold
and stars lie on the stiles like snow.

The robin came with a silver bell
in his black silk throat
and thin legs made from sticks and thread,

an imposter bird I was right to dread.
A real bird would have called the trout
to the mossy shore among roots and leaves

and belled the cat that chased the mouse
that spoiled the milk
the cow had made. A real bird

would have sung a worm, a sun, an earth
rising from the sea in praise,
green waves breaking hills of wheat

the stars had made of my black dread
that all my years are dreams I made,
that all my houses have not been home

except to time and its belled pet
that rises with the world and sets
when stars hush in sun-split trees.

Jack is dead. Jill lays flowers
on his grave, and I alone have never heard
the bell that chimed when the brindled cat

pounced on mouse and bird
and world and time began to dream
this last long drawn out word.

October 4, 2002

Destiny

There is a way of doing things
and a different way of getting the whole
thing wrong, and sometimes they are the same.
The fence a man nails up is the fence that pens him in.
Right now I'm getting used to that.
I've often said, do it wrong, for God's sake,
take down the house, shovel the road
out of the lake, roll up the fences
that cut the plateau up and walk through grass.
Feel that grass become the sun.
That was then. Now I think I should
have left God out of it and done it right,
built another fence of grass, of wind,
so when I took it down, as I hope I would,
the empty night would gleam with stars,
the moon would fall into my mouth and speak
tonight this earth, this mind, this first
downed scent of snow that blows
across the trees for a thousand miles until it is
stilled where there are no fences but ourselves,
that fence — what? I don't know.
I stare across. The barbed wire sings.

HAROLD RHENISCH

lambs

cken
here,
l
aisies

ou like,

blackberries bloom, lichen
devours stone and sheep
flock as sheep will,
for the dead are not
dreadful, and the soil does
not taste sour. Come,
you can drink it here
in the dark malt, in pasture,
the light that shifts
through grass in shape
of stem and halm, the sun
that is a point of cloud
that swirls and thins,
and in the hand I proffer you.
Come, pull me up
and I will be son, father, friend,
friend, father, son.

Bach-wen Cromlech

Look at the shape I'm in.
I am crouched under a low

doorway made out of stone,
and stars are pressing down upon the roof.

I have lost the shape I was and have not
yet found the new shape of this place,

except it rushes forward and retreats —
I remember that from the old life I lived

with wife, daughter, dog, and the big
house above the sunflowers

that I was always painting, over and over,
as my heart beat. That's it, it was a heart,

and I fed it well — wine, apples, meat.
I kept in shape for it and it

pounded every minute out flat until I found
myself here a long way from home,

the touch of lichen on my fingers, the cold
of wood upon my cheek, the burn

of water in my ear and the high cold
air rising to the sky where once

there were stars but now
is only the shape of things to come.

Finding Ourselves

You are telling me to learn the word
and then to speak
the house, the home — they are both
the same, you said, and smiled,
but I would rather listen to the long
quiet speak itself with such strength
as words can give to it, or us,
who are listening here
where words are home and we are strangers
at the gate who've come to ask
for knowledge, love, but find instead
release from meaning, and reverence
for what we must yet work out —
neither in words nor in the steps between
the words, that echo here, on the porch
where we shuffle, cold,
in the sound of distant traffic
that fills the city with a hush
but in the river falling from the mountain,
bright with trout and orioles, that roars so loud
we hear nothing else.
What words contain can't be given,
not here where the door is black,
the knocker brass, and opens wide,
nor in the house where we're at home,
although this is not home for us
but a house we visit when we're in town
and find ourselves
as distant strangers, close friends.

Harold Rhenisch   21

Plato's World

If it is true there is a world of forms,
where every leaf is the light that burns
within the leaf when the sun
strikes poplars in the afternoon,
true that all light is darkness
etched into form by a dreaming
mind that cries out a world then tosses
into silence, its mouth
stuffed suddenly with tongue and teeth,
its Word splintered into words,
tiny, crowded together
if they are to mean one short,
snipped thread of the impoverished
world, if it is true
that love, hate, and suspicion
are shadows on summer grass,
that there is a world where each is
squared out of cut stone
that is not stone, where you walk
in a shape that is not you,
where I don't wear these hands,
these eyes blinded by a knife
of light thrust through glass,
these calloused feet, scarred knees,
chainsawed thumb, then the colour
of these trees, yellow as a robin's
beak, is real, and lasts. If there is no
such world, it passes. A fly settles on still
water in the last light; a trout rises. Long
after the sun goes down I'm still
standing at the window.

Meditation at Samhain

We sit and watch the candle
burn through this still night
as we talk across the narrow space
under these stars that have fallen
low against the earth,

a space as dark
and distant as the night
you died, the day I was born, but near,
so near we reach across
and touch, not you

or I, but us, and nothing. Nothing.
There are times when nothing
is bounteous. If this were time
this would be that time,
but it is the earth where time
is not and we are talking us.

Don't stop. The dark
is vast and though I know
that what we stare into
is that part of what we speak
and touch not yet touched
and spoken only

in the way you speak and I hear,
I reach across the black —
that came before this was —
as long as staying lasts,
the candle burns,
and words are speech.

Look up. Against the sky —
green as a leaf — black
trees bristle with the cold.
It is that sky we talk.
It's not words we speak
but speak through

and art is not to contemplate
a dream of order but order
that has no bounds,
no rules, except that in all this night
that stretches, vast,
above the pines,

that bough and sway
beneath the weight
of stillness, it lingers.
It is what we can touch,
not the clotted, snarling earth,
but the burning stuff

within the flame,
the place that's still
and where we cross
from where words burn us
to where we, trembling, touch
and never ask what it is that burns.

Welcome

I am building a house.
You may move in
if you like. I have moved in already,
among the workmen,
who I do not see.
I say this to be frank.
There is something more than house-ish
about this house,
something that makes it home and hearth,
a house to make love in
or to dream
as the floors wheel with children
and the moon rolls
from window to window
like glass
as I pace from dining room to hall.
I do not feel alone. Do not think that.
Sometimes I feel a wind
blow over heather from a sea
that is not here,
in the mountains.
Sometimes the walls whistle
like bone. Maybe it is the workmen.
I have gotten used to that.
You will get used to it, too,
since you have moved in with me already,
it seems,
and the squealing children,
the banging doors and empty halls.
You will see (or not); the workmen,
if it is work they do,
or some pleasure
that looks like work to me,

Harold Rhenisch   25

don't get in the way. They never do.
It's worse. They aren't there,
or here, if this is where,
or near, or even far,
as most things are
far when seen up close,
yet every night another wall is plastered,
windows are set into empty frames,
doors hung, tiles laid. Maybe
you know the doors they've entered
in the air, the ledge they sit on
to eat apples and drink coffee black,
the clapped shoulders, the clanking
tools, the sun that sets on their long
walk home to houses of their own,
which is why I have invited you,
that you do know enough of that
and know the square of a house,
what passes in and what should be kept out
at all costs.

Pruning the Tree

There is a tree above the glass
behind the kitchen.
I prune that tree while ghosts watch
from the attic window
where I slept last night, a guest,
undisturbed, yet changed
by what passed or did not pass
between dream and breath
in that cold bed. Streaming
through panes of glass, the moon
set the room at sea
where waves rise up to spars
and fire burns on rope and mast.
Whales breach and dive,
trailing stars in the cold
depths where now I work
in a thin sweater in the face of storm
to cut off twigs and shape a tree
that was never shaped except
by wind and summer sun,
shading those within
the house who carve out words
with camel brushes and have now
gone from this earth — or into it —
as have house and tree —
leaving me here, still in the wind,
to shape a tree shaped once only
in the falling year. It has some years left.
I see it through to fruit
while ghosts watch from the light.

Harold Rhenisch   27

Walking Riddle

I am walking across a moor.
The skies are dark with cloud.
There is a dog, no path,
and an apple in my pocket.
I have never been here before. I don't
know the way, what town
I started from, if there even is a town,
or a farm hiding from the wind
behind a hill, or when I left,
or what's my goal,
if I am expected
or when I can expect to turn the corner
and walk down the lane to the red door.
Stars don't wheel above my shoulder.
The sun doesn't rise or set with wheeling
birds and thin fog caught by trees,
yet it doesn't feel as if I've just begun.
It feels as if I've always been walking
on this path, as if the moor
is so real I must cry it out with every
step I take, leaving my self
farther behind in that earth
I press with the print of every heel.

Old Photographs

There is a box with photographs
on a high shelf white with dust;
the earth that seems so solid
is only time which passes — not
to any end but to begin, with man
and woman first, then children,
the years of art, the long years after
when worship ruled the house
and music, played as memory, moved
the mind to set word on word
the way a house is built from wood and stone
but also from intent to build a home
and shelter from the years that pass
as pictures until they lie in cardboard
on a high shelf as children run
in and out through another sun
built not of words but of their intent
where men live still and women
laugh as waves crash down,
or where children come for reunion
across the scattered years a man builds
up and leaves as record for himself to live
once only. The mind is air.

The Fire

In the garden there is a fire
that is ashes now
and drenched with rain
in which wine was poured
and forgiveness asked
for presumption,

in which praise was given
for the gift of words
that, opened, fly into the trees
and peck at seeds
which fall and sprout
as trees.

Branches in a green book
burn my hand.
I will not pick it up again.
The man is dead who lit the fire.
It seems so strange a thing
to say a man is dead

who danced with kings
and walked the bridge
between the stars,
who loved the earth
and all the pictures
we call men, the art itself

that we call women,
the leaf that flows
within the twig, the crow
that steps between light
and dark, the song
that calls itself the song.

Such a man is not dead.
Dead is only what we knew
when we drank wine
and broke bread,
breathed smoke
and named ourselves

the moon, the stars,
the freezing grass
that whispered underfoot
our art, and all
we understood
as what we are we are.

A Game of Chess

When asked to heal, the words we set
on the checkered board

angle across to the other side
where each is found

where it was not, leave fields
behind and black

forests, rich towns, mills
and weirs and children running

in packed yards of sagging
stables, pounce and scheme,

build sacred halls, tear earthworks down,
fall maimed or dead or damned,

or worse, the realpolitik of a mind
facing blindness and the beautiful queen

across the gulf of what it knows
but can not heal. Healing is a different art,

the hands thrust into autumn soil,
the knobs of garlic like buried stones

that once were eyes or hungry mouths,
clammering together in their sleep,

the dreams that come from long patience,
that come in crowds of breathless absence

that do not ask and do not answer,
rook and bishop, knight and queen,

pushed aside as the king steps
from his keep at last to answer

the charge of his own presumption
and receive the death

of life in her long mirror
or praise in ours.

Spell for Adoration

If the mind is woven of the sun,
the sun of the body passing through the wind,
the wind of dust, if straw can see
and weave the sun from grass
and twig and stone, if you press
your forehead to the coolest earth,
tasting mountains' thinnest sap,
drink, and do not look for sense.
I do not describe a land, but enter one
between land and this you enter
from the other where that gives us name.

If the oldest world of magic is within my yes,
if the alder, birch, water, sky, the snow
are passed hand to hand to tree to rock to leaf,
if we move through root, stone, pebble, rain,
and repeat ourselves by singing wave, fish, grass,
freshet, and sing our path before our breath,
if out of endless night, if water, oar, breast,
stone, hand, mouth, flame, these figures
cast the foxglove earth and earth's a spell
cast on us, I do not have a self, nor you, but we
are lovers drinking water by a starlit window.

The Whole Cloth

When I said the goddess walks down the red
hill to the sea that eats the shore,

I was walking down through gorse
and a flood of bees to salt.

The taste of each word on the tongue
was a sting. When I said that God flies

above black water, stars
spilling around Him like foam breaking on a beach

where long-legged birds run,
I was standing in deep water,

among kelp forests full of herring
as whales brushed my cheek like birds.

When I said that man and woman lie
in bed as swallows dip and whir

in yellow light, moving as shadows
passing through the day, I was bed

and swallow, tasted man and woman,
and sang your dancing wing. Body,

earth, and mind are threads
in a cloth I wrap around your shoulders

in the cold night, as snow rivers
underfoot and the dog ranges through black trees.

Harold Rhenisch   35

The Tower

Locked in a tower of bleak stone
in a barren land
where he once had fought for freedom
by speaking of the heart
in airy trills, a sacred bull that plowed the land,
of heroes, queens, and the crippled poor
who had inherited their green
earth, and made of it a pasture
and a graveyard, a senator of the land
he made, in fact, much honoured, praised
for beauty, wit, writes of golden
birds that sing in towers locked
in time above a black sea.

Those who listen to such birds,
to decipher the poems they sing (if they
are poems), or warnings (if they can
warn any man enough from his own folly — the one
to which he opens his house),
do not hear his words, only birds
riding thermals above the tower,
only dreams of a man lost in time. They do so
at their peril. They are not poems.
They do not sing with clockwork
timed to match the stars,
have no gears or springs,
and make no sound. They are not warnings,
for no man will hear such
warnings; if he did
he could not heed the world they made,

which is his own, where stones
fence meagre fields and must be broken
down ahead and built behind
if a man can pass and not be walled
with only stone and sky and a country
green as grass. The sea is black.
It is not time, if you thought of that.
Time is another trial, another passage
we must take when going back.

Burning Sticks, Mallorca

Two old friends
swagger out,

their bellies full
of meat and drink,

to make a fire
of olive wood

long past the months
of blossoming.

The stars are bright
and cast a smoke

across bare fields
where every step

turns up stones
and whispered words

we pass like breath
from the teeming

earth beneath our feet.
Are we that earth?

Not exactly.
It is more like the day

between dawn and dusk,
the oaken hull

bored by worms
between sailors

and the sea
that wants in,

you can be sure of that.
Two men walk back

across the years
to cast a spell

to bring white blossoms
to almond trees,

ewe to ram,
thought to no man,

to be most hidden
and alone,

and linger there
on that windy ground

the way a mind
fixes on a thought

and shakes and will
not let it drop.

We speak it all
in leaves that catch

the wind or even
stones that rattle

under our feet
but speech is not

what we spoke
before we faced

the nameless face
of our own end.

In life we are alone,
locked in trust.

It's death we share
with men, like this.

The Teacher

A man is born
in a sea and dreams
of trees and mountains falling
in swells of stars
breaking in foam,
and then is set
in a white room
and told to teach
those who come
from their own births
with their deaths
in hand
as he has his own
behind him now,
a black hand resting
on his shoulder
as he speaks
what must be said
but he does not know.

What can any
man teach to those
who know as much as he?
It would be better to learn
the silence they break
by entering the room,
or how to speak the night
their shadows know,
which lies between
each word he speaks
and deafens him
to all their pleas
for poetry. Really,

he can teach only
the simplest things,

the way a body
becomes a word—
except they would stay
outside the word;
how a poem can speak
a body, or fan a love,
or bring a child
to life on earth — except
they would think
he spoke a poem.
And yet he must begin.
He is in the room.
Nothing can be taught,
he begins to say,
and then looks around
at faces
washed with light.
We can only forget ourselves.

The Well

I've spoken to you so much
it's time, I think, to say
just what it is I've learned from you.
We could begin like that,
or we could be more direct,
hissing that we haven't even exchanged
names, let alone letters, and to tell the truth
it's I who's done all the talking
to this point. I wonder
if it always ends like this:
at first the shock, then excitement,
fear, the loss when we're apart,
the grey empty years, waves
welling from a sea so vast
I stand on the shore, as tiny as a crow
hopping among broken shells —
not there at all,
seen only by the space where I am not.
What is that space?
Clouds tower and combers
thunder three miles out.

Harold Rhenisch

The Truth

Tell the truth, you said;
I told what I knew,

but for the life of me I can't remember
what I said,

the story of the child I found
among the trees or how the child found me

and I told the men who came
with dogs

what she said before she died
in my arms and the world came

crashing down
in waves.

Do with me what your justice says
that you must do who look for truth;

I never saw the girl before; now the girl is you,
who've bought her memory with my blood;

I only pray
that you will have an easier time

among the trees and will know who's who
when asked and who you are you are.

I can't change that,
just as I can't bring her back

to tell the story of the man
who dragged her off

among the birches with rough words,
or the other one,

how she was watching light
filter down through leaves

and got lost.
We all get lost. It must be that.

I'm lost right now. Aren't you?
That's truth enough.

The trouble comes
when men find us there

and give us truth
that we don't want or need.

Twenty-Year Poem

Whenever crows fly overhead
I see one bird as black as grief

balanced on its scaly feet,
dropping a stick from chestnut trees

where you walk, white-bearded, slow,
in a March wind,

twenty years ago,
when you looked up

as light and branches wove and unwove
and flowers burst.

You were struggling to find your way back
from a world you found the night before

that had no shape,
and all the other worlds of other nights

from which there might
not be a single path

that leads to you
or me or us. I need to know

if you made it back,
sold your black coat and black hat

at a flea market, how large
a sky the crows fly through,

who are a passage,
not a shape,

and where you went.
It must have been only half a world,

the way you kept coming back,
just like I speak for half of us

when I sound like both.
A full world has no shape.

I think this might be where you came
and where I left.

You will know me
by the crow that squawks

when you hobble down the walk,
a flower in your lapel,

and laughs out loud
as it drops the stick.

I will know you when I see you
raise your cane and swear.

Nothing

I come in tonight from iron trees
and marigolds — once saffron,
now black, crumpled —
because your light was on
and cast a shadow on the street

where I passed, lost
in thought. I am only nothing to fear,
for fear needs shape and breath
and there are no words for nothing
as nothing really is — except

for everything, and that is far too full
and incomplete. Something
will also just not do. Birds
and leaves rise in the sun
in nothing, and fall in nothing, and it is

not the same as the empty well,
the broken town, the amount
you owe the grocer for the fruit,
how much you won at cards.
You were a man, if it's to the man

in you I speak — if not to woman,
god or goddess, or child,
who also wander in your bright halls,
following the echoes of your words
and deeds. The old phrase is the best.

Living or dead you were up to something
until I came with nothing much
and made a fuss. Now
you are up to nothing too
as you listen to my listening.

You speak what I mean
more or less and everything
you may have thought is now
so full with light that you forget
I wear no mask but the mask

I always wore when I was alive,
the face, the hands, the voice,
my fingers stained with cigarettes,
my teeth broken with whisky,
my beard uncut. You wear it now,

as if you wore yourself so lightly
as flowers grown from earth,
and, inside out (if it is to the face
of you I speak), or crumpled up
(if it is to the heart,

where pith is green and smells most bitter),
have become the world that speaks us out.
We are not apart and flow like wind
slamming up against the glass,
and if that is nothing that you expected, for me

it's really something and means everything.
I raise my glass and give you thanks,
and in mine see yours,
already drained as the ice knocks about
and chills the whisky on my lips.

Harold Rhenisch   49

Belief

I do not believe
that what I know

of what was said
by the first word

I spoke or was spoken by,
the water and the rain,

the window and the wind,
can be said,

but know belief
is strong enough

to break the spell
I cast across

the self that knows
the words it speaks

make sense,
and tell the world

they know the name
I am and if not name

then thing, belief,
or water running down the pane.

We must be known,
or there is no belief

in this that speaks our unbelief
in truth or world

or the moment when
we knew at first

we had been found
among the last lost things

of a world that speaks
a language of itself.

There must be sense
and nonsense

to create the trust
that carries us

from puzzled doubt
to sure knowledge of our ignorance,

where no belief or unbelief
can rescue us

from the selves we've made
to speak for us

in the empty world, the trees,
the grass, the flowing wind,

and this which speaks
the little we have become to be.

Harold Rhenisch   51

Coming to My Senses

I used to think that fire was hot,
water wet, and the grass
that blew along the dike
was dry and rattled
with the sound that echoed back
to the rites of earth,
the planting of the seed,
the harvest of the grain
under turning stars
and chill wind,
that what was certain
was men, and women,
and the lives they made
on sacred earth,
the touch, the kiss,
the four posts of a house.

I thought to make
of this quick life
a tower I could climb,
with water, air, and fire,
to make a rite of earth
that would give me passage
to the world
such words describe.
I was free, bound
only to what I thought,
and what was that
I don't know now
that I've been burned by fire,
drowned by water,
and have walked as grass
that grew as a man

out of the sand
along the dike
of this river we are
and are spoken from.

I have spoken
to no-one about this,
until now, with you.
Don't blush
or roll your eyes.
I don't speak
because I trust you
more than the others —
we are all strangers
to each other —
but because I see now
trust is not needed here.
There is something living
that is not us but lives us.
You are the darkness
I want to have a word with now.

How It Was

The tales must be told and retold
or they're not tales: the woman lost at night,
the falling cliff, the rising sea,
become cliff and sea and corpse
and not us, who tell our children
how it was when pigs flew, grass was green,
and what a man spoke had meaning not just
to himself. A man must be told
that he's not rock, not wood, not salt,
a cry that falls, a woman missed,
and not the hiss of waves that swallow
us below the cliffs or he will not walk
into the dark where rocks rule, salt
stings, and no man or woman's
cry is heard by those who stay
inside, not calling, not
telling tales we all must listen to.

Falling Stars

She told me she had never seen
a falling star so I looked for years
to see one drop across the night that is older far
(though what is age when we move together like the tides?)
than the cities we have built to name the paradise
that we have left or entered every night we wake.

The tide that's out will soon come back.
The world's a book that, opened, is not read
but lived or journeyed (which?)
or put in doubt. I see a dusty road
between low hills. Ahead there's Jack,
chopping ladders that lead to heaven,
which are not ladders but a crop
in a plot behind the house
while all the government's five-year plans rot.

Stars fall, my love, and with such speed
that in the moment I cry, Look! I am too late,
for when you turn the sky is dark
and there's only Jack, who has an axe.
Mercifully that's when we wake;
we don't hear the pages turn,
see Jack's giant fall or feel the earth
crack and break and the blackest
sea come rushing in.

Harold Rhenisch   55

The Craft

Teaching children to sing as rain streams down glass and trees
bend, leaves fly, clouds crack, and all
you have at hand is memory of how you began to sing
when birds came to the planes — flaring words —
to eat the blossoms for a day, and then were gone
to a long summer of wind spilling branches and a world of smoke,
is a lot like learning to balance silence and a footstep,
melody and dust swirling up from gravel, branches, and a tree.
The body is our life; with its hands we touch breast and lip,
thigh, buttock, or even tousle the heads of children, raise
their chins, set them in rows above an altar and lift their voices up.

Even as we talk, lake and air that form a shore outside the song
have become the walls that echo the voice that sings
(rustling paper, black notes in even bars). When we step
up to the window, to wipe the rain aside and see
out to the storm, we sink to our feet, trembling;
a face stares back, pale, streaked, and thin
as light: water driven by storm. The trees
that bend flow within the frame
of cheek and chin. Eyes blur with leaves. Hair flows down.

The world is slow; slower still is understanding.
Behind you voices drop from a cold roof. You are stranded
within them and all the years when singing came
instead of birds that you had lost; you do not turn
from birds that shoot through a haunted face,
beating wings heavily against a wind,
because you can't explain the way you stare
as if not there. You aren't. The children are.
They will learn in time. Here they teach
the way to listen when you are singing children.

The Hidden One

It is difficult. I want to tell you
of the fire that drives the tree
out of a grove of darker trees,
but know it's less
a talk of poplar, maple, ash,
the sun that burns
upon the earth,
than talk of standing still
so that one afternoon
of sun in leaves
is all the world.
I don't have words
in mind at all,
and I did, and don't,
yet I have begun
with them,
despite myself.
I don't know how
I will smooth things out.
I think we poets lied.
What should I say?
That we wrote
when we were drunk,
that the ground
we walked upon
was only love,
that the sun
was not in the sky but within us
and did not rise
and did not set?

Harold Rhenisch   57

That would be too much
all at once,
yet where else
does a story start
than at the end: the hero
ruined, his house
razed, poplars
springing up in fields
where no cattle graze.
From there the earth is no excuse,
nor are we.
Once we get here,
it is different ground
we walk upon,

but how would I explain
such walking
when words delight in hiding,
and even now they're hiding
me from you
behind the trees.
I drink the light
in the world that trees reveal
and speak with you,
despite my self
that waits for me to
return with a single word.

The Parting

I am moving out.
My things are packed.

The taxi's waiting
on the street.

 I brush my hair
off my cheek

and shed a tear
for what we almost had

and dab it off
with a folded tissue.

My lipstick's smeared.
I smile, to put

myself at ease, turn
quickly now and run

down the steps.
I don't look back.

As the taxi fades
into a hiss,

the ivy clutches
the black wall,

the windows fill with ink
and you turn back

to your moonlit rooms
where centuries pass

in the moment
you take to clink

Harold Rhenisch   59

the ice cubes in your glass
or smooth back the sheets

or just walk
from moon to moon to moon.

The floorboards creak.
The room smells of the sea

that rocks our grief.
I didn't know your name,

and you don't know mine,
if there is a name for us,

together or apart,
and I won't think of you

except as the one
who found me

as I found him,
naked, blind, unshaped

in this formless place
spelled out by fingers, lips,

where in all our hurry
we must rest.

Don't think of me
in another's arms

in Moscow, Tel Aviv,
London or Toronto,

because there are no
other arms than this

that reach out
and, so, reach back.

Moel Tryfan Quarry

To leave the garden,
the stream, the singing

rock where water runs
beneath the path,

binding leaf-black
gate and slate that once

held fire in the household,
black iron, hunger,

and now cups rain,
nettles, and heron light,

for walls of stone
where mountains fall

into deep pasture
with no bottom

except the blue
fog where man

and woman, red door, child,
find themselves

as names and name
the world alone,

speaking mountain,
air, fire, smoke, the chill

of mind that finds
too soon the end

of reason and reasons
the cold returns

to seek the still-
ness man is,

without knowing end
or beginning,

is to roof the mind
with sheets of slate

brought up three
hundred feet

through blue rain
that fills the pit

where men once worked
to shelter earth,

knocking stone
from stone

to build stone up
into homes a man

can now buy with credit
and not own,

the dead cars holding love
in the back seat,

and how you fall
when first you stand

high on the tip
and throw stones down

into another life
that holds your fear at heart.

A Proposal

I don't know enough of the seas of light
that flow down through the windows

to explain to you the currents there,
or why our houses don't burn up,

why we aren't ash, why water puts out fire,
except perhaps they are too similar.

Of a woman's love or the breath she takes
when waves break and rocks shudder,

I don't know enough, nor of the slant
of light through blinds I open now

to face a wind through grass, and close to face
whatever we said and can't unsay,

though I can't remember what it might have been.
Of the words, the simplest words

that come between us and name us you
and me and our love hate I know too much

and would forget them but there's no forgetting
that you and me and hate and love

were all said and all spoke our minds.
If we can't remember what they meant by words,

let's learn instead with fingers, lips,
warm breath and hair drawn across the chest,

what words spoke when they meant us
and we cried out, astonished into life.

The Spoken World

Since every word is a splinter
of the word God spoke,

or speaks, because the world
is not past but with us,

pheasants startle out of grass
in a dead vineyard,

a hawk sits on taut wire, cicadas
cry, the sun beats down,

although it often seems
it's yet to come; the sun

that rises over larches
rose yesterday and once again

we will face it, if not
wiser, touched by the sense

that we belong on earth
and what we say might

reflect our place, it should be no
surprise that broken bones

can be healed, children
whispered into life, a lover's

sadness cured, by words. It should
be no surprise,

but is, at least,
relief, that something

of this world still unfolds
within music, as we unfold

in bars and staves,
breves and cross breves,

in time and measure,
the blossom from the black

winter bud, the fruit
from the blossom,

the laden branches
touching grass.

Why then should we not
speak, together,

of what is most
intimate: the way

we move together,
and moving, still.

It is a spell we cast
upon the forest trees,

the house that breaks
around us, the black

air rising up,
the dizzy stars.

The Island at Dawn

The proudest man moves to an island off a coast
where trees are fog and gold is pounded
to hang from ears instead of laws and writes, alone,
to forget all books, all pride, as if words could wake
as grass rising from a morning tide
and the stink of salt that comes with dawn
could be written down and remain in dream,
where islands drown and men crawl onto sand
and gasp and cry and trample flat
salt hay and grass. It can't be done. Pride
can't turn back the human need for stone
that gives the body bone, nor water,
which rains within our limbs. Salmon spawn
where we return with dawn to die, yet do not die,
though die they will when they won't come back.
Tiny silver flashes flow down the streams
into the sea, and men come crawling out and gasp
and groan and spew out salt and see it cold
for the first time: the stony beach that
they must cross to reach the shelter of the trees.

The Witch

In this story nothing's true.
There is a witch, but she doesn't heal,

bind lovers or lead the rites
of death and birth, the hawthorn

blossom or the pippin apple fallen
in the wind and falling snow

now dark in starlight
on the edge of evening

in December. She does not walk
under the iron boughs

of leafless trees, with the green
grass of April in her fingers,

and is not the trees that rake
in triumph at tattered skies

to claw the moon into her nest
and scratch its face

with the pain of love. She is no celebrant,
but a twisted fear given breath,

her dugs shriveled, her tongue sharp,
her nose a hook, her eyes a hate,

a crippled thing, but dangerous;
mock her not, but praise her strength

for strength is weakness without love.
No life can begin where life

is not given but is taken, cut
and buried deep within the dark.

I tell the truth that lies will mock
as false. Beware of truth, but do not mock

it falsely, or it will turn and call you back
to the hag who lives in a hut

and burns the forest of deer and birds
into coal. The wind that howls

around the chimney is less to her
than the words she burns

to feed the story that she is,
the ending she will become

of all that do not believe
the truth she lives, and to keep her warm.

For her the wind is cold. Do not mock.
The world she makes

has the strength of words and fire,
the choking smoke, the red

eyes of the ones who rise to Heaven
on the fear of men who blaspheme Earth

to make a god of words that speak.
Words don't speak. No men

walk the fields at night, only men
and women walk to the dance,

to dispel words, break up their charms,
banish belief and pray the captain

keep his trust, all guests are safe
in our wild house, the king shall live,

and the woods stay planted on the hills.
If you be not true, then all love is false

and the worlds we make will char
us into coal that will burn again

to ash and grow cold,
and you will be false before the year is full.

Facing the Light

They say we're born,
or born again,

born in the wrong time,
or not my son,

my daughter,
or must be adopted,

the way we carry on,
or born too soon,

came out backwards,
caused too much pain,

or refused to come at all
and were cut out

and brought like that
into the world

we say is born again
in every minute

and is our birthright.
We say that, too,

it is our birthright,
hoping to make new again

what has grown old
and stale. We bring

ignorance into the world
and nurture it, praying

that it will remain
ignorant of what we do

and we have done,
that the world we've lost

will stay with them
who we have borne

and birthed and brought
to face the light

we all must face —
that the world is lost

and we are all
that we can face —

praying that some day a world
we can touch and feel

may be born from that,
facing us at last

to ease us from fear
into knowledge,

knowledge into wisdom,
wisdom into ignorance.

Making Sense

Although it makes no sense at all,
we have the right to place this word

upon this word, making our way
with stuttering steps

back to the beginning of all right,
where all the words —

these autumn fields, brilliant skies,
cattle in the yards, white and red —

have fallen off and only one is left,
then is silent and a bird

flies over dark water, then fog,
and night, and have sense

enough to walk backwards into the door of time,
to look back and see behind

but not forwards where we will be
more broken into words,

howls, scratches in the throat,
glottal stops, whispers, clicks

and all the languages
that make sense of us.

Sewing the Self

The hills of stone
stand within

the rocking sea
and hold back

sheep a small
child speaks

when sleep and star
count the time

between each
slate laid

upon each hearth
when sleep won't come.

The hills are cold.
I walk there now

as now walks me,
but dare not

count the sheep
that leap the gate.

None of us
are what we expect,

I know, but this
is hard. The sheep

stare through stiles,
the gap between what is

by being us,
unasked, unaided,

drawn out through
a needle into cloth,

dressing us, not up
but down into

the time we spend
walking the lives

we have always
known we are.

Earth

Each rock is sacred.
I put this stone

upon this stone,
red with iron,

worn down by rain,
to build a wall

and house my love,
with her grass hair,

her lips that move
around each word

she mouths
to speak a home,

as this is home
for us and this

whole time we have
spoken is all the time

there is and time
enough to share

a life, children,
dogs, oxen,

the pastured sheep
and horses walking

Harold Rhenisch   75

up the slate hill
to bring down stones

which I set here
upon this rock,

making of words
and taut muscle

one moment
on which words break

and answers tumble
to the very ground

we speak and speaking
lose again to gain our selves.

Equilibrium

I live there now, if that's what it is,
the way its plains are thick with trees,
field follows field, tightly fenced,
all marching off in even ranks
to a horizon that swallows them
into more fields, more trees,
more mountain ranges worn into seas,
thrust up again, wild with rain.
I have raged against the war
that comes from deep within and breaks
these beams like straw, and falling fire
and cities going up in smoke.
We say a fire rages, not that a fire
has gained equilibrium.
We keep that for water, the touch of thirst,
the edge of the knife that becomes the plum,
the autumn that sheds cool days by the stream,
the chill balance between cupped
hand and mouth, the point at which
water leaves water and becomes blood.
Afternoon sun slants in through pillars
where priests once walked and took their air.
We come down from the senate and dispense the law.
The plebeians are rioting in the streets.
We slip back home and make our poems
on our wide bed, quoting poets now long
since dead or exiled in the East,
living on the edge while light falls in sheets.
But is it water? Can't water rage
and fire be the equilibrium that some men seek?

Call it rage, the shape of things to come,
or love. It is what we shed
to be here for a moment where all
love is lost and passion found
before we are brought to court and made to speak
that word we flee. It is our sentence and our judge,
and the only window in our cell.

Fate

It comes to this. At first, a cradle
rocks, a hand brushes, a cheek
whispers, a lip opens to speak a word,
and then the child is schooled to stand on the wide earth,
with nothing in its hands or on its lips,
the cradle hung from an attic beam,
and must learn to tell the one long story that we are,
of king and queen, the princess in the tower,
the prince who stumbles across the moor,
the sea, the forest, the shining sword that cuts the knot,
and the others who also tell the only story
but know it not and hound us to hell and back,
to wrest it from us, as we must break it from their hands,

although once we've travelled to that other
place there often is no coming back
to sea or forest or woman's bed.
The story ends, the cradle's smashed,
and we must live it endlessly; it's not ours to give
to any child with hand or lip because we haven't
told the end of it. It may as well be there is no end
to what we tell of this one story
that stains our hands with blood
when we would love and praise
the earth and all who set us on our path,
but if we love we must walk this path
on this only earth. It comes to this.

Messages

The thought I have is not my own,
but is the thought that moves earth and air,

and is the fire that burns within the tree,
the stone, the leaf, the bird.

I am the silence thought glides through,
the unexpected pool between dark rocks,

in shadow, cool, while on the slopes
the day blows hot, hawks hunt,

and pines burn down to light.
In the darkness when I dream,

I am not the dream that pours
through me like water

emptied from a pitcher — clay —
into a cup, ringing out

as it strikes itself at last.
The world is music.

I am not the cup, but the passage water makes
from itself to its other self

which becomes the first water of the earth,
fire of the sky, breath of my thought.

Of this I know. I only answer
the knowledge that I have.

What I do not answer
is the message that I bring,

the answer you send back,
from where it came

or where it's going next
to find itself at first

or what questions it should ask
when it comes at last

as now it comes
and we who listen are the speech,

the falling rain,
that passes through us

to the river,
river to the sea, sea to rain that,

falling, is the answer
we should ask.

Full Stop

I am always stopping. No sooner
do I start than I put on the brakes,

slam into the dash, hit the wall,
when I need a break from trying to begin,

come up short, totter on the brink
and stare into wrecked cars

down by the creek, or sit
and leave the shovel in the hole,

the hammer, nails, and saw,
lying on the wood in spring sun

as vines reach for the light,
and catch my breath, which, I tell you,

is hard to catch; no sooner
do I take a breath then I must stop that too.

My whole life's made of stops like this:
the street that ends at another street, the page

that turns to stories that start and stop,
one page a minute,

numbered, chopped,
and sewn against a spine. A book's

a lot like a man: no sooner
do you know the lovers, who bumped

who off to marry whom (in books they talk like that)
then the story stops, the ends tied up —

roughly, no doubt. You are left lying on the beach,
in your own life, stopped in your tracks.

You look around: sand, water, bodies,
just like yours, oiled, burnt, perhaps bored

and looking for a way to stop the thought
that this is it. Your heart stops.

You must start at the first page again,
stop, the second page, stop, and go on,

this time without surprise until you stop,
exhausted, and know the second start

is no start at all, once you have stopped.
The light, the night, the day, the rain, the wind,

these all stop, as does the snow, the love,
well, maybe that is at last a start,

though I have known even love to stop.
Still, stopped,

it lingers, makes you wish you could say
those words again, not the ones that stopped

the kiss right on her lips but the others
that stopped the start so love could begin.

Sometimes I stop and look over the cliff
at the hayfields and the river

and my breath stops,
and when it starts it is a different breath.

Sometimes I just remember it.
It may be so with all that stops,

the story I make up
in fits and starts, the one you hear

as it echoes where I stop and you begin
to breathe again, set down the cup,

lift the words, your lips, the cloth,
as I begin to stop myself.

The Old Poet in Venice

The water pools at the house's root
and black ships pass through walls of stone
mirrored in the tide. In a house's attic
a man lies alone, condemned to silence
by his pride and the words he's made
to turn all gold to love, a childish trick
he used to win a war long lost
before it began, as it should have been:
war's unjust, and tides rot all wood
that holds all houses above slick mud.

The sun breaks in as curtains,
drawn for distant guests, are pulled
from glass that rings with sound
of birds and streets where bridges cross
stagnant water and people dress
as who they're not. For just one day
the prince is poor, the orphaned girl
a priest with robes and golden mace,
a poet a boatman who guides a boat
from here to there but never back.

There is no going back. A man
knows that when a man is lost
within himself and the city's name
is all he has to answer back
when he is called to sound himself
upon the drum and can make no sound
except the burning pride of having loved
and fought with words, praised tyrants,
become a fool and accepted pardon

when he should have screamed
to the heavens that in this world
there are only fools; we dress
in masks and take for lovers those
we know not and cannot know. There is
no turning away and no going back.
No heaven gifts us words like that.

Snow Scene, with Dogs

I strike out across
the fields of snow

and words come too,
on leather traces,

snapping fish,
when the sun is gone

and ice thunders,
heaves, cracks,

and breaks apart
in the howling dark.

And you, who are the snow,
that blots out South

and East and West,
not white but dark,

where do we travel
when we leave our camp?

I need to know.
The sun comes once a year,

and when it comes
it stays; blue sea

rises through the cold.
Then you are gone

Harold Rhenisch   87

and cannot answer.
It's now I need to know,

how far we'll travel
before I shoot your dogs

one by one
and gnaw their flesh.

North is no direction
but where we are.

What lies in snow?
The man who walks alone

without dogs or sled
is not a man

but that which comes
before he took that shape,

a single breath
frozen in the air.

The Looking Glass

Did you hear that winter's over,
the ice is melting and the birds

are coming back? They asked,
and I ran to the window,

and, sure enough, goldfinches
in the swaying elms were plucking blossoms

from the twigs
and the glass surged in the wind

that pressed against the house,
and so I learned what people meant

when they whispered *winter's over*
and say that now to be in that house.

They say that glass is liquid
that takes a hundred years to flow

from the top sash to the sill.
You knew that, in that house.

There's nothing in this world
that can be told to anyone

who doesn't know already what
you would tell

or that you told it
long ago by asking what they knew.

Harold Rhenisch   89

That's why I tell you this,
about the question, the golden birds,

and the glass that has flowed now
halfway to the sill

and whispers winter's over,
when it's just begun.

The Questionnaire

I'm at my wit's end,
trying to talk as the wise once talked,
through questions answered,
answers questioned,
and doubt used to mock
the institutions of the state,
the cock that crows at dawn,
mentioned not to repay
a debt but to make a loan,
not that they don't need mocking —
they do, always — but that
the mockery has brought me
to endings now, the groan
of a cracking ship,
the spreading slick, the U-Boat slipping back,
not to the start of things,
which is where I need to be
if I am to begin as a man
and not as a thing they made of one
to do their work without question.
In this play in which we star
it's your turn to mock me now,
to ask what work was done
unwillingly? Oh, it all was willing.
Let me write that down
in the blanks between the words
that you have left for answers
to the questions that you lead.
I pitched right in, dealt
words out like a deck of cards,
swept cards off to chart a convoy,
the beeps and pings of escorting
ships, the silent speed, because

they told me to get in the fight.
I fought. I don't have the strength
to question the questions you answer
me with, because I can't
answer my own answers with applause.
I'm coming to my wits end now,
and if I've found you in this place —
at least I think it's you, though you might
be someone else I used to know
when I was the man they thought I was —
I'll speak your language, though haltingly,
hear your answers and smoke
your cigarettes. Do your best.
I have no questions.

Unlocking the Key

I have locks on all my doors,
locks on my car, my bike, and on my mind,

and I have deadbolts, chains, keys, and sliding bolts
to keep my thoughts from what's out there

and wants in here where it's warm,
music plays, and children sleep

where they must be safe
or there is no shelter in this world,

no space to think and lose
our minds and be the space

that we lock in
and locks us out.

I am sorry. Now you're locked in here
with me, my children, and my wife,

and you must watch
as we cook our rice,

make bread, or love, and our scent
fills the house, the children

stir, remembering what was, and you
are embarrassed or want to watch,

but the door is locked
and you are only house,

lock, children, music playing,
the keys that lie

still on the kitchen table,
and not us, and cannot see

what we touch, or feel the parts
we see for us

where there are no locks,
no you, no us,

but only the children,
as we walk out

and throw the jingling
keys into the grass.

The Report

The reports keep coming in
from men who're walking to the pole
across drift ice, bridging cracks
in ice with sleds, shooting dogs
and bears, and lying in the end
when they return to cameras
and champagne — if it can be said
a man returns to the man he was
before he left or if he can leave
himself behind as he travels
into ice and what he cannot say.

It is a journey no man can make
or no one takes because the route
that's mapped is not the path
one man breaks, frostbitten
and sick to death. Not one
of them arrives, yet their reports
keep coming in, as if we who stay
behind, or say we do — for no
man stays a moment in this place —
could read the cold in black and white,
small figures etched in snow and freezing
half to death, and not just lies
which are only truth seen without belief.

We reached the pole on this day —
or one that men write. We don't
think we have the strength
to make it back. Each man tries it for himself.
We feast each one on his return,
file their reports and do not tell
them that the men they are

are not the ones who left. We tell
them instead we are not the ones
they left behind and let them smile
and tell us again how far they've come
and gone as if a man could tell
the truth or believe it if it lied.

Distress

To shake off dreams
that filled the house with dread
I would run out at night
under the moon
as the wind blew through the naked
branches of the trees,
a dog at my heels, the first snow
crisp upon the grass, and feel
the world tower to the stars,
and would laugh and jump,
or fall down into snow, but now
it's memory and far too real.

Now it's not me that runs,
but the trees and snow,
and when I look up through the branches,
I am the dog,
panting hard, the branches,
twisting, shifting, black,
and the stars that scatter in the oldest
bridge between the living and the dead.

I am looking down from that high
bridge over an orchard
in the snow in which a boy tries to shake
off who he has been told
he is for what he knows he cannot
reach and will never touch
except right now when boy is tree and dog
is star and all sway
and blow and fall apart, scatter,
drift in a fine
wind over a crust of snow

the boy runs through, oblivious
to us who watch him fall
and get back up and run into the house
where sleep replaces sleeplessness,
and are now alone among the trees and writhe
beneath the turning stars.

I am Fighting

At first it was brother,
father, God,

who made the world,
He said. Then it got hard.

I began to fight myself,
right hook, left jab, and well-aimed kick

(Penalty! Against the rules!),
bounced off the ropes,

and lost my teeth as cameras flashed
and bets were passed,

and still I fought for a father's love.
He was the ref. I passed him cash.

The odds were set. I couldn't lose.
A hundred ancestors sat around in black,

and passed the bets, trading marks for rubles,
zlotys for crowns,

until one whispered I should throw the fight
or I was dead.

I looked around. They looked aghast.
I guess they'd seen enough.

I won that fight. I'll retire, I said.
I didn't know what I know now: no one

retires from the fight.
Now I am fighting them.

They crowd around
with schemes for building

town halls, railroads,
and an opera house,

pass me papers,
ask me to sign,

right here, right there,
pass me a pen, paper, ink,

and smile. Or spit. Some spit.
My credit's good, they say,

and nod. They all nod,
a thousand shadows

stretching back. My God,
I think, some day

I'll come with dollars
to the fight and sit

with them, my red
beard grey, and trade

for pounds and pesos,
francs and yen, hold it up

in fistfuls and wave and shout.
I am fighting that.

Rage

We call it rage, the water
rising within our swollen words,
the sandbags banked against the walls,
the cattle trucked to higher ground,
and we, who are the banks,
willows, reeds, and rotten tires,
the dikes of cars and rock trucked down
from mountains made in fire,
crushed by ice, shore up what was said
and could be unsaid, like this, which says what truth
would hide and hides the way each word,
each breath we take, flows in,
flows out, and floods the blood
with pounding air. This
is the rage — that all the words
that flew like geese above the fields
as snow blew white through
yellow leaves and skeins of ice
were not water and water not words,
that leave us here, alone,
as flood rises, sandbags break
and all our rage is loosed
across the fields and streets we
sought by this, with this, to protect.

It's Greek to Me

I studied Greek and learned the words,
the Greek of man, of fate,
the woman whose hair is snakes,
my daughter's name,
cicadas singing in evening light,
the sea — the dream of sea —
charms of passion, and war,
frightful war, the farm, the town,
the place where power starts
and we all belong to black soil and grain
as rain falls and earth drinks.

It's Greek to me, people said, meaning
reason, or not meaning,
what Plato wrote, what his master asked,
what no man can answer
except with death, where we are honest
and where we lie with a straight face
for once, as I am lying now

where I die into my life:
the Greek of lead,
the type too small to read
to show the blanks where words
will be in the finished book
that we lay out now to see its shape,
its weight, and how it feels
to hold it in the hand.

Grass Dance

We say it is green, I'm in the clover, the grass is greener
on the other side, but do not say the ochre
stalks of fall collapse with frost and rise like flame
from glacial clay.

In this space I've cut between house and trees
I speak of grass before it goes to seed,
although the greenest plants — dandelions, clover, cress —
are not grass, and the tallest
are over the fence, and though I call it home, it's not.

It is a place we stayed until the sun fell behind the hill.

Harold Rhenisch studied poetry with Robin Skelton and P.K. Page in the 1970s. Since then, he has published twenty-six books, including ten previous volumes of poetry, as well as fiction, memoir, bioregional essays, translations, environmental photography books, and reviews, and has edited both of Skelton's posthumous books of verse. *The Spoken World* is his eleventh full-length collection of poetry. He is the winner of the Malahat Review Long Poem Prize (twice), the ARC poem of the year prize, the CBC Literary Prize for Poetry, and the Theatre BC National Playwriting Award. He is an editor of poetry, fiction, and nonfiction, has taught poetry and short fiction at Vancouver Island University, and his multiple-genre workshops at the Victoria School of Writing are legendary. His *The Wolves at Evelyn* — "a hybrid of creative non-fiction, autobiography, historical narrative, and philosophical treatise," according to *Quill & Quire* — won the 1978 George Ryga Prize for Social Responsibility in British Columbia Literature. Harold Rhenisch lives in Vernon, BC.